The SAMARIA GORGE

**A complete guide for travellers...
with 102 colour photographs
and maps**

MICHALIS TOUMBIS EDITIONS S.A. - ATHENS

© Copyright 1998   MICHAEL TOUBIS PUBLICATIONS S.A.
                     Nisiza Karela, Koropi, Attiki
                     Telephone: +30 210 6029974, Fax: +30 210 6646856
                     Web Site: http://www.toubis.gr

ISBN: 960-540-009-X

*No one who has not walked
the gorge of Samaria
and the plateau of Omalos
can say that he knows Crete.*

Foreword

In some of the most magic moments in the formation of the universe, nature bestowed rare beauties on the Earth. Only the works of nature can put such majesty before our astounded eyes. One of the greatest of those moments was when the Samaria Gorge came into being, with all its wealth of wild grandeur. The sharp contrasts in its terrain, the rare species of plant and animal to be found there and the exotic nature of the landscape all fill the traveller and scholar with unique impressions which will stay for ever in the memory.

The Samaria Gorge has been described as the most magnificent in the world. It was no coincidence that the Council of Europe has awarded the area its Diploma First Class, as one of Europe's most beautiful spots.

The picture revealed by the early morning sun as it rises to imprint the shape of the White Mountains on the dense mist, is one of pure magic. The pines rustle, the water chatters over the stones by the springs, and the birds sing amid the foliage and the pine needles, charming our senses with sound and colour that blend with the scent of wild flowers and rare herbs.

The book you are holding is our attempt to help you get to know more about this fascinating natural wonder. We have collected facts and descriptions from bibliographical sources, from research on the spot and from the stories of local people. We believe there is something here for all those interested in the Samaria Gorge, and that our book will be of use to the visitor. It is, after all, no coincidence that the people of Sphakia say, "There is only one gorge: the Samaria Gorge! All the rest are just ditches!"

Contents

Foreword 4

Geographical description 7

Geological description -
morphology 10
Flora...12
    Dittany 13
Fauna 15
    The wild goat..............................15

Traditions and legends....................20
MYTHOLOGY................................22

HISTORY..
Archaeology - antiquity...................23
    Tarra 26
Period of Venetian rule 27
Period of Turkish rule....................28
The German Occupation................31

YESTERDAY AND TODAY......33

INTRODUCTION
TO THE TOUR..............................43

Map of the main route 42
Chania - Omalos plateau 44
Omalos - Xyloskalo 48
Instructions for visitors 54

Table, map and
instructions for the main
Xyloskalo - Ayia Roumeli route 56

Ayia Roumeli - Loutro -
Choria Sfakion 78
Chora Sfakion - Chania 80

GETTING TO KNOW
THE AREA AROUND
THE GORGE 82

Xyloskalo - Gigilos...........................82
    Seli Gigilou - Volakias...............84
    Seli Gigilou - Achlada -
    Koustoyerako..............................84

Omalos - Kallergi 86
    Kallergi - Pachnes 86
    Kallergi - Poria - Psari -
    Melindaou 86
Omalos - Psilafi 86

Xyloskalo - Kladou Gorge.............87
Xyloskalo - Tripiti
Gorge..87

Ayia Roumeli - Souyia....................88
Ayia Roumeli - Elygia
Gorge..88
Ayia Roumeli - Angelokambi 89
Ayia Roumeli - Gavdos 90
Ayia Roumeli - Ayios Pavlos -
Loutro - Chora Sfakion 90

Sfakia - Anopoli...............................93
Sfakia - Frangokastro......................93

Index...95

Geographical Description

The White Mountains (or 'Sfakianes Madares') occupy a vast area and contain 57 peaks of more than 2,000 metres. The tallest is the summit of **Pachnes** (2,453.65 metres), the highest mountain in Crete after Psiloritis (2,456 metres).

It is only natural that such a place should have numerous ravines between its peaks, and the largest of them is the Samaria Gorge. The length of the gorge is 13 km (along the path from Xyloskalo), or 16.7 km as far as the coast at Ayia Roumeli. The area around the gorge (totalling 4,850 hectares) has been declared a National Park. It forms part of the province of Sfakia in the Prefecture of Chania.

A number of other ravines, most of them impassable, lead into the Samaria Gorge. The rain water and the run-off from the surrounding peaks when the snow melts drain into the central river, in which there is water all the year round. When there are cloudbursts during the winter, the level of the water rises sharply at certain points, and the gorge becomes impassable because of the force of the water and the stones and pieces of wood it carries along.

The main path through the gorge runs beside the river, which walkers must cross 47 times before the foot of the gorge. The narrowest part of the gorge is towards its southern end (14.30 km) and is called the **Iron Gates**: here the walls close in to leave a gap of only three metres. The cliffs rise sheer for 300 metres on either side, to a final height of 700 metres.

The Xepitiras cave (see p. 82).

During the first few hours of the walk, as we descend from Xyloskalo, we are in the deep bed of the ravine, with its conglomerate rocks. Everywhere along the route are the aged trunks of water-loving plane trees, which seem to be trying to hold themselves upright by thrusting their roots ever deeper into the ground so as to resist the force of the water during the torrential rains of winter. The water in the river-bed often disappears, and where it bubbles up again it forms small watercourses below which the water gathers in little pools. In their surfaces are reflected magical images of the surrounding mountains and trees.

In the gorge there are 20 springs of water, which the public authorities do their best to maintain for the use of walkers and to make accessible to the birds and animals which live in the National Park. Among these springs are those at the spots known as Linoseli (at an altitude of 1,500 metres, on the way to Gigilo), Neroutsiko (below Xyloskalo, on the way to Samaria), Petachteni, Potistiria, Myrties, Kavousi, Loutsopo, Vroula (from which the village of Samaria took its water), Kefalovrysia (where the water wells up in considerable quantities from the river-bed to provide water for Ayia Roumeli), Perdikas to Nero, and Vourlia (from which the villages in the gorge got their water).

The gorge contains a large number of caves, most of which are unknown to visitors and provide homes for birds and animals. There are also countless smaller ravines, some of which are called Strefomadi, Potistiria, Yermata, Kalokambos, Avlimonakas, Volakias and Prinias.

Geological description - morphology

The geological upheavals of the early Miocene epoch, 25 million years ago, led to the emergence from the sea of Aegeis, a continuous stretch of dry land which linked south-east Europe and Asia Minor. In the middle Miocene, 18 million years ago, Aegeis had high mountains and also dips filled with water. The flora grew to such an extent that by the late Miocene (14 million years ago) Aegeis was inhabited by large herbivorous mammals. But in the late Tertiary period (10 million years ago) the waters of the Mediterranean began to inundate Aegeis, forming the islands of the Aegean and Crete. Eight million years ago, Crete was already surrounded by water. In the Pliocene epoch (1-3 million years ago) there was a constant process of rise and fall of land, and a deep tectonic rift was created in the Cretan Sea, approximately in the same position as it is today.

Geological upheaval in the area once occupied by Aegeis continued throughout the Pleistocene epoch (1,000,000 - 25,000 years ago), in which there were successive warm and cool periods caused by the gradual spreading and retreat of the glaciers. As a result, the level of the sea rose and fell, creating bridges between Crete and the adjacent lands over which the island was colonised by animal and plant species.

Today, southern Crete is 3.65 metres higher than the north of the island. The line of the former sea level can be seen clearly in the steep cliffs along the coast.

Scientists believe that these upheavals were caused by the pressure which the African plate exerts on the European plate.

The Samaria gorge was created during the Quaternary period. The dolomite beds of which the rock formations of the area are composed have been fractured by a variety of factors (glacial action, karstic phenomena, etc.), which are particularly marked in the Gigilos area and around the Iron Gates.

With only a few exceptions, the flora and fauna of Crete have remained unchanged since very early times. In the Minoan period, the climate was slightly cooler, favouring the development of the local flora and fauna, a process which reached a peak during the period of Venetian rule.

When the Venetians left Crete in 1669 and the island came under Ottoman control, we can assume that the inhabitants moved up into the mountains in search of safety. As a result, the forests of Crete were destroyed to make way for new pastures. Unfortunately, this process of deforestation has continued down to the present day, and the woods and forests on most of the Cretan mountains have been burned off.

The streambed in the gorge is often broken by the ancient trunks of water-loving plane trees.

Flora

The Samaria Gorge and its surroundings contain a very wide variety of species of tree, bush and other plants, some of which are unique. The vegetation consists largely of tall cypresses, many of them centuries old. The villages of Samaria are surrounded by olives, from whose fruit the local people extracted oil. In ancient times, the forests in the gorge were worked systematically (see History: Antiquity). Under the Venetians, Tarra exported timber for the construction of the fortresses of Chania, Rethymno and Herakleio (Handak). At this time, there was a water-powered sawmill in the area, which was still there under Turkish rule (the last reference to it dates from 1876). The pines of the gorge produced large quantities of bark, resin and firewood, and continued to do so until the gorge became a National Park in 1962.

The medicinal and aromatic plants which flourish on the Omalos plateau and in the gorge are of the greatest interest. On the peaks around the plateau, the **ambelitsia** (*Zeltova cretica*) grows in abundance. This is a bushy plant with hard wood whose branches are used for making the strong and long-lasting staffs and walking-sticks essential for shepherds and walkers on the wild, difficult paths of the White Mountains. The Omalos plateau is covered with dense undergrowth consisting of largely of chicory (both *Cichorium intybus* and *C. spinosum*) and other plants. The medicinal plants marjoram, mallow and dittany are particularly common.

Dittany

The most important endemic plant in Crete is **dittany**, known locally by a variety of dialect names such as ´erontas´. This is a bushy plant found nowhere else in Greece, but which grows in the ravines of the Cretan mountains.

In the Samaria area, it is abundant in the Ayia Roumeli entrance to the gorge.

Dittany is an evergreen plant with small heart-shaped fleshy leaves, light green in colour and covered with fine white hairs. It is very difficult to pick because it prefers high place, where it grows in the cracks of tall, steep cliffs. It is known for its therapeutic properties: according to the ancient writers, wild goats eat dittany to heal their wounds. Its scientific name is *Origanum dictamus* or *Dictamus creticus*. Although it is aromatic in its wild state, the aroma disappears if it is transplanted into a pot. In fact, there is a myth that Zeus deliberately planted it here among the rocks, and that when anyone moves it he becomes angry and deprives the plant of its scent.

According to the myths, dittany was dedicated to the goddess Artemis, because both it and she helped women in childbirth. That is why statues of Artemis were often decorated with wreaths of dittany.

Many of the writers of antiquity mention dittany, including Homer, in the *Iliad*.

Hippocrates, the father of medicine, makes a special reference to Cretan dittany and its therapeutic properties.

Dittany.

The wild goat chews dittany to heal the wounds of arrows (D. Dapper, 1703).

Sage (*Salva officinalis*) is a bushy plant with elongated narrow leaves of a light green colour. There are two types, the domestic variety (with a slightly broader leaf) and the wild kind. Sage produces a type of oil which is used in perfumes and essences and for medicinal purposes. Like many other medicinal and aromatic plants, sage is used in Greece to make a winter drink.

The **mallow** is a bushy plant with numerous tall shoots which, at intervals, form clumps consisting of many small tightly-folded leaves. It is light green in colour and the leaves are boiled as a winter drink.

Marjoram (*Origanum majorana*) is an aromatic and medicinal plant. The essential oil produced from it is used in the making of soap. Marjoram is used to make a winter drink, either on its own or with mallow.

Chicory (*Cichorium spinosum*) flourishes throughout Crete and is abundant at Omalos. This bushy, thorny plant is eaten raw as a salad or boiled. When dried, it is placed across the mouths of jars used to store water, to prevent insects from entering, and this is the source of its local name, ´stamnangathi´ (´jar-thorn´).

The famous honey of Samaria and Ayia Roumeli owes its incomparable quality and taste to the pine trees, the **thyme** which is to be found everywhere in the area, and to the heather which clothes the mountains around Omalos, Samaria and Ayia Roumeli.

Above: sage; centre: marjoram; below: Phagnalon ruprestre.

Fauna

The Samaria Gorge is one vast nature reserve, and a paradise for the animals which live there. Wild goats, snakes and birds all inhabit a unique landscape and help to make it one of the most beautiful places in Europe. The smaller birds are to be seen at every step. The gorge itself is full of **partridges**, usually to be seen near the many springs - one of which, indeed, is called ´Partridge-water´. Predators of all kinds live in the steep cliff faces, including **hawks, owls** and **ravens**, while the proud lammergeier rules the higher peaks.

The lammergeier (*Gypaetus barbatus*) is the rarest of all the birds in the gorge. Only a few score pairs have survived in the White Mountains, most of them in the ravine next to the Samaria Gorge (the Kladou Gorge), where they are protected. Their bloodcurdling cries can often be heard among the towering cliffs.

Among the other large birds to be found in the vicinity are the golden eagle (*Aquilla chrysaetus*), which preys on wild goat kids, lambs, hares, etc., and the vulture (*Gyps fulva*), which lives on carrion. It has a wide wingspan and a bare neck.

The gorge also attracts populations of migratory birds, including **turtledoves, quail, woodcock, hoopoes, thrushes** and **swallows**.

Numerous small animals live in the gorge: **polecats, badgers** and many **hares**.

The Wild Goat (kri-kri, agrimi)

However, the best-known animal connected with the gorge, today as it has been since antiquity, is the **wild goat**.

Its figure has appeared in works of art by ancient and modern artists, and the wild goat makes frequent appearances in the folk songs of Crete:

Wild goats, oh, wild goats
and gentle deer,
tell me where you dwell
and where your winter grazing lies.

Our lands are the mountains
and the ravines are our winter grazing,
and in the tiny caves among the cliffs
you will find our mansions.

The wild goat of Crete (*Capra aegagrus*) is a ruminant (belonging to the family of the *Artiodactyla ruminata*).

Those who wished to hunt them had to be almost as fleet-footed as the goats themselves, and the hunt was very tiring. When the Cretans wanted to praise someone for his speed and skill in walking the cliffs, they would call him ´goat-footed´. It was regarded as dishonourable to kill the females or the young.

The Samaria Gorge, together with the neighbouring ravines of Elide, Kladou, Domaton and Trypiti, is the last part of the island in which the wild goat lives free as it has always done. In former times, it was found all over Crete, as we can see from the surviving place-names: Agrimoschisma, Agrimokefala, Agrimochorafa, etc.

In the early morning and then, to a lesser extent, in the evening, the goats come down to drink at nearly all the springs along the gorge. The forest rangers and forest fire patrolmen have got into the habit of feeding them by hand, as if they were tame, in the yard of the forestry guard-post at Samaria. This is a good time to photograph the animals.

The wild goat's only real enemy is the golden eagle. In earlier times, the gorge also contained a kind of wild cat which preyed on the kids, but the last specimen is believed to have been killed by a shepherd in the 1930s.

When the wild goat realises that its end is near and that age is weighing too heavily on its body, it withdraws to an isolated spot and dies. Indeed there are those who believe that there are goat graveyards in the mountains.

Thanks to the protection afforded by the state, there are now several thousand wild goats - which is important when it is remembered that not many decades ago the species was in danger of extinction.

High up on the steep cliffs, the Cretan wild goat is almost the only inhabitant of the gorge.

It is chestnut brown in colour, with a darker brown stripe running from its neck along the spine down to its bare tail. The males are larger than the females, and have a black beard. The males sometimes weigh more than 40 kilos.

The horns of the male wild goat are long - up to 70 cm. - and may be as broad as 5 cm. at the base. Along the length of the horns are knobs from which it is possible to tell the age of the animal. Each age of goat has its own special name in the local dialect.

In antiquity, the people of this area made bows out of the horns of the wild goat. The men of Sphakia, in fact, were renowned as the best archers in Crete.

The wild goat is extremely agile, and when necessary can leap huge distances across gullies and ravines.

In ancient times, the wild goat was sacred to Artemis, goddess of the hunt, who was worshipped in Crete as Britomartis - that is, ´sweet Virgin´, from ´britys´, ´sweet´, and ´martis´, ´virgin´. As can be seen from a funerary column from a temple in Chania museum, Artemis was also known as ´Diktyna´.

Among the myths with which the wild goat is connected is that of the birth of Zeus, who is supposed to have been suckled by the goat Amaltheia in the Idaean Cave. The two nymphs to whom care of the infant had been entrusted, Ide and Adrasteia, used to pour the goat's milk into a horn to feed him, and thus it came about later than Zeus, out of gratitude, made the goat's horn - the ´cornucopia´ - the symbol of wealth and the multiplication of good things.

´The Upbringing of Zeus´, a woodcut by the important painter and engraver Kostas Grammatopoulos. The two nymphs, Zeus and the wild goat can be discerned.

Detail of the Ayia Triada sarcophagus, showing wild goats.

The wild goat is mentioned by many ancient authors.

In the *Iliad,* Homer refers to the bow of Pandarus, made from the horn of a wild goat (translated here as ibex):

...Straight he uncas'd his polish'd bow, his spoil
Won from a mountain ibex, which himself,
In ambush lurking, through the breast had shot,
True to his aim, as from behind a crag
He came in sight; prone on the rock he fell;
With horns of sixteen palms his head was crown'd...

(*Iliad*, IV. 120-125, trans. Lord Derby)

Wild goats are a common theme for depiction on ancient vases and coins, and this gives some indication of their sanctity.

Scenes showing wild goats also appear on Minoan sarcophagi, on seal-stones, on coins and in paintings on walls and rocks.

faience wild goat
the Minoan period;
ossos, 1600 BC
erakleio Archaeological Museum).

Traditions and Legends

The traditions and legends which have survived about Omalos and the Samaria Gorge sprang from the difficulty which humans encountered in explaining the wildly varying terrain and the unique landscape. The strange sounds which are to be heard as echoes distort the rustling of pine needles and the peculiar shapes to be discerned on the towering rock walls in the strata of geological upheaval stimulated the imagination of early man.

The unexplored and inaccessible caves, the tall, unscaleable rocks whose shape changes completely as night falls, the streams which bubble up in one place and disappear in

another - all these features went into the creation of a magical world of gods, demi-gods, ghosts, fairies, dragons, demons and nymphs which the local people inherited from their forebears or made up for themselves.

As the walker descends the narrow, winding path among the tree-trunks of the pine-shaded route through the gorge, he will see the wide, often snow-covered rifts of **Gigilos** and **Volakia** and will experience a sense of fear lest the huge rocks towering above him in various places, seemingly ready to tear loose, should actually fall into the void. The name ´Gigilos´ is derived from the ancient Greek ´girgilos´, which meant a pile of stones.

It is still said that Gigilos is the haunt of demons and evil spirits. That is why the local people fire off a weapon when passing the spot, to scare away the spirits. Even now the older people of the area wish that someone they dislike may "go to Gigilos".

There is no end to the legends about this place. It is said that among the towering, lonely cliffs of the Samaria Gorge lived evil spirits which were the sole residents of the area and had sprung from the incision made by the Titan's knife. Those who entered the gorge fell prey to the evil spirits, who were also capable of eradicating any trace of the unhappy travellers.

One day, though - so the story goes - a fossilised fish appeared on the wall of the gorge, with a cross next to it; these symbols drove out the evil spirits, and since then it has been possible for humans to pass by.

MYTHOLOGY

According to one of the myths, the Samaria Gorge was created one day near the beginning of time by a Titan, one of the earliest Cretan gods, who drove his knife deep into the bowels of the earth. The kings of Crete went into the gorge to sacrifice to their gods.

Near the impressive cliffs of Gigilos, in the direction of Omalos, is a large natural platform. This is said to be the place where Zeus drove his chariot, or where he descended from the sky in his chariot to wash in the waters of the *Linoseli* spring.

The cave near Linoseli, known today as *Daimonospilio*, contained an oracle.

The cave has never been explored, and the sound of rushing water can be heard from its depths. It was said that fairies lived in the cave, and according to local shepherds music can still be heard coming from it.

Near the church of St Nicholas (before we come to the village of Samaria) was the site of the ancient city of **Caeno**, where the goddess Britomartis (or Artemis Diktyna or Cretica) was born. She was a Minoan divinity of the forests and the hunt, and she protected the flocks. Britomartis had a special affection for the wild goats, with whom she dwelt. Always depicted as very beautiful, Britomartis was the daughter of Zeus and Carme, who was herself the daughter of Euboulus and thus the grand-daughter of Demeter (see the *Greek Mythology* of Kakridis, vol. 3). Britomartis loved to walk in the forest and to hunt. When she is distinguished from Artemis, the myth has her as the faithful attendant and companion of the other deity. When King Minos saw her, the story goes, he was dazzled by her beauty and fell madly in love with her. He chased her for nine months up the mountains and through the glens, but she always managed to escape him in the forests. But in the end he caught up with her on the brink of a cliff, when her dress snagged on a myrtle branch. To avoid capture, she plunged far down into the sea, where she fell into the nets ('dictya') of some fishermen. That is why the Cydones called Britomartis 'Diktyna'.

Another myth tells us about Apollo, who after killing the Python sought expiation at **Tarra** (modern Ayia Roumeli), where rites of purification were performed by the priest Carmanor. There Apollo fell in love with the beautiful nymph Acacalis. Overwhelming by his feelings, he fell asleep in her arms - so Pausanias tells us in his description of Phocis - and left the earth in darkness. Indeed, this is one explanation of the darkness in most of the gorge. Acacalis gave birth to twins, Phylacides and Philyndrus, who were suckled by a female goat. That was why the inhabitants of the ancient city of Elyrus dedicated a bronze goat suckling two small children at the Delphi Oracle. Carmanor was appointed priest of the temple by Apollo, and later became a prophet and hierophant.

Ancient Tarra had a lake with a tall cypress in the middle, which disappeared beneath a landslide. The local people say that beneath the lake was a huge hole, from which there is a current of cold air even today. It is said that the queens of Tarra used to bathe in the lake.

Aphrodite, Britomartis and a wild goat, in a relief.

HISTORY

Archaeology-Ancient History

The archaeological interest of the Samaria Gorge area increased considerably after May 1990, when a forest ranger discovered fragments of terracotta vases and two terracotta lamps near the church of St Nicholas, which according to one school of thought was the site of the ancient city of Caeno. The finds were decorated with stars on the lower part, with, above, the upper part of a young female figure with long flowing hair. A bronze arrow-head and a small bronze ram were also found. These were votive offerings, according to the historical evidence, and they lead archaeologists to the conclusion that they were dedicated to the sanctuary of Apollo which we know was located somewhere in the vicinity. Excavations continue, and it is hoped that they will produce evidence on which safer conclusions can be based.

The ancient city of Caeno is placed somewhere around the church of St Nicholas by the historian Rushley. Theodore of Sicily says of Caeno that *"They say in the myths that Britomartis, known as Diktyna, was born at Caeno in Crete"*. There is, however, another school of thought which says that Caeno was not a city at all, but the name of a mountain or a cave (Paul Faul).

The site of the ancient city of Tarra was fixed in 1959, with the finding of numerous fragments of glass vases, testimony to the existence of glass-making workshops. This important archaeological investigation was funded by the Gorning Museum of Glars (*Cretan Chronicles* XIII, 384).

Tarra was one of the 100 cities of which Homer tells us. It stood on the site now occupied by Ayia Roumeli.

The English traveller Rushley was the first scholar to identify the position of the city. It took its name from the root ´tal-tar-taur´, which means a gorge with a river at its bottom, and it is mentioned by numerous ancient writers. According to Deffner, the city had a temple to Apollo: Stephen of Byzantium tells us that: *"Tarra is a city of Crete in which Apollo Tarrius is honoured"*.

Archaeological excavation has demonstrated that Tarra existed as far back as the Late Minoan period. In the museum at Chania is a stone column with the double-axe symbol, dating from historical times. Among those whose descent was from Tarra were the scholiast Lucillus (2nd century BC) and Chrysothemis, son of Carmanor, an athlete who was victorious at the Pythian Games. Tarra founded a colony - by the same name - in the Caucausus, and some scholars believe that ancient Tara in Lower Italy was also colonised from there. Tarra formed an alliance with the cities of Elyros, Hyrtikis and Lissos; the alliance issued coinage showing the head of a wild goat on one side and a bee on the other. The cities exported timber to Egypt and Knossos, where it was used to build ships. It also sent massive wooden pillars for the construction of palaces at Tiryns, Mycenae and Troy.

According to Svoronos, the Dorians made Tarra a populous and important centre. In the Hellenistic period, Tarra and its allies Lissos, Poicilasos, Hyrtakis and Elyros formed a league with shared civil rights under the title of the Koinon of Oreia, with its capital at Lissos (to the west of Souyia) and a common religious centre at the Diktynaeum of Lissos.

Excavations carried out in 1959 in the graveyard of Tarra produced jewellery of the 4th and 5th centuries BC. The city was particularly important during the Roman period, although it was destroyed - according to Deffner - in 66 AD when the south-west coast of Crete rose by 3.65 metres.

Tarra lay on the sea route from Rome to Egypt and the East. Merchant vessels laden with wheat stopped there to take on supplies, or to shelter in its harbour from the storms of the Libyan Sea. Glassmaking developed in Tarra at this time, and continued to flourish in the early Byzantine period. Its position now favoured its growth still further, for it lay on the sea route between Egypt and Constantinople. The importance of Tarra continued down to the 6th century AD, when it went into decline as the wheat trade between Egypt, Rome and Constantinople became less significant.

During this period of commercial importance, the inhabitants of Tarra became ship-owners - building their vessels in their own timber - and engaged systematically in piracy. These activities came to an end in the 7th century.

Among the possible reasons for the decline of Tarra are the raiding and looting of the Arabs, a change in the sea routes, natural disasters (earthquakes) and the abandonment of the urban centres because the economic relations among the population became rural in nature.

The Period of Venetian Rule

The village of Samaria was first inhabited under the Comnenus dynasty of Byzantine Emperors. Early in the 14th century, members of the Skordilis family from Chora Sphakion moved to the village. There was a reason for this: the commander of the Venetian guard at Sphakia had tried to kiss the beautiful ´Chrysomalousa´ (´goldilocks´), of the Skordilis family. She resisted, and he hacked off one of her golden tresses with his sword.

The Skordilis family was determined to avenge this insult, which it did by wiping out the entire Venetian garrison and their commander.

The Venetians attempted to force a passage up the gorge to punish the Skordilis family, who took refuge there, but in vain. In the end, they were forced to come to terms, under which the beautiful Chrysomalousa became a nun in the convent of the Blessed Mary of Egypt, at Samaria; when she died, according to local legend, she was buried with her gold loom. Throughout the period of Venetian rule the gorge was the haunt of freedom fighters, and the wind of liberty and disobedience to the conquerors blew through it. After the failure of a rising in 1570, Provedatore Marino de Cavalli ordered the destruction of Sphakia.

An engraving of Sphakia.

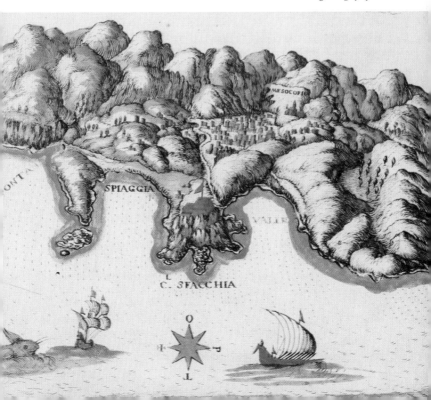

Among other references to the area in Venetian times is that of the traveller Bellon, who, visiting the island in 1546, praises the ancient Cretan cult of Artemis:

"*It is no mistake to say that in antiquity the Cretans worshipped Artemis. Even today they instinctively continue that old custom. They are trained to proficiency in the use of the Scythian bow in childhood*". (Quoted in Simopoulos, *Foreign Travellers in Greece*).

The Italian monk and pilgrim Noe wrote that: "*The Cretans can stand much hunger and hardship, and they are fine archers*".

The Frenchman Jacques le Saige tells us that: "*The Cretans are artists of the bow, and the arrows whistle when they leave the string*".

A medieval Sphakiot archer.

Turkish Rule

In the great Cretan revolt of 1866, Omalos, the Samaria Gorge and Ayia Roumeli were mustering-points and places of refuge for the revolutionaries. The supplies sent from mainland Greece to Crete (Ayia Roumeli) included a complete small printing-works, together with a printer called Ilias G. Manios.

After many wanderings and adventures, Manios settled in Samaria and in January 1867 printed the second issue of the newspaper *Crete*, which supported the rebellion.

The Commission of the General Assembly of the Cretans had its seat in Ayia Roumeli, and it formed a Provisional Government there under Parthenios Peridis. Ayia Roumeli was also the location of the main foodstuffs and military supplies warehouse, stocked by vessels sailing out of Piraeus, Syros and elsewhere. In December 1866, Mustafa Pasha sent three warships to bombard the foodstuffs and military supplies warehouse and the shore at Ayia Roumeli, where women, children and wounded revolutionaries had congregated in the hope of getting safe passage to mainland Greece.

The day after arriving, the Turks landed a boarding party and a battle ensued, lasting many days: in the end, six hundred Turks were killed and the remainder were forced to retreat.

In July 1867 Omer Pasha landed 4,000 troops at Ayia Roumeli and the Cretan revolutionaries were forced to blockade themselves in the gorge, taking with them as many supplies and as much ammunition as they could and setting fire to the rest. Omer

failed to gain entry to the gorge, and burned down Ayia Roumeli instead. The ship *Arkadi* was taking on women and children in the harbour when it was attacked by two Turkish vessels. It fled, but later ran aground off Palaiochora. Most of the passengers survived. In 1868 Omer Pasha took Omalos, but the revolutionaries soon drove him out again.

By 1869 all of Crete was back in Turkish hands, with the exception of the Samaria Gorge. Three hundred revolutionaries, with leaders from all over the Prefecture of Chania, struggled through a long winter against the snow and appalling weather, without hope of obtaining supplies from anywhere. In the end, they were compelled to surrender.

Cretan revolutionaries.

A battle at Ayia Roumeli.

Daskaloyannis.

In the early years of the struggle against Turkish rule some of the most important events in Cretan history took place in the vicinity of the Samaria Gorge. In 1770, during the rising led by **Daskaloyannis** of Anopoli, 4,000 women and children being pursued by the bloodthirsty Turks took refuge in the mountains: most of them in the Samaria Gorge, and some in the other ravines. They were saved by the stout resistance of Yannis Bonatos, whose force of 200 men held the Iron Gates and eventually forced the Turks to retreat.

In 1821, the whole of Greece rose in revolt - unsuccessfully, in the case of Crete. Once again, the defeated revolutionaries were forced back into

Cretan rebels with Hadzimichalis Yannaris.

the gorge - and this time all the Turks' efforts to capture Omalos were in vain.

One of the leading figures in the movement for independence from the Turks was **Hadzimichalis Yannaris** from the village of Lakki, Kydonia (see p. 47). Since Lakki was the home village of many revolutionaries and the starting-point for much action in the cause of freedom, a hymn to the struggle of Crete for liberty contains the following lines:

...One the one side the men
of Selino and Lakki
and on the other, into the fire,
the men of Sphakia...

Hadzimichalis Yannaris was chief of the armed bands of Kydonia from 1866 to 1898 and President of the Cretan Assembly. He took part in all the risings against the Turks and set up numerous raiding parties to attack them. At one point, the Turks forced him to live in Constantinople, but from there he managed to escape to Russia. In 1864 he took the initiative for a meeting at Omalos of all the Greek dignitaries of the Prefecture of Chania at which a denunciation to the Sultan of the atrocities committed by Hekim Ismail Pasha was prepared. In 1877 he returned to Crete and in 1912 was the President of the Cretan Assembly which proclaimed Union with Greece. He died of natural causes in 1916.

The church of *St Pantaleimon* at Omalos (Lakiotikos Yiros) was built in his honour, and the *Tower of Hadzimichalis* stands there.

The German Occupation

After the attack on Crete by Hitler's troops (20 May 1941) and the retreat of the joint Allied forces, the Greek Government and King George escaped via Omalos and the Samaria Gorge to Ayia Roumeli, where they embarked for Egypt on 23 May.

The Germans placed a strongly-manned guard post at the entrance to the Samaria Gorge, in the hope of being able to prevent the movements of the Allied undercover units in the area, whose task it was to collect information and dispatch it rapidly to Middle East Headquarters. The Germans often sent out raids from Omalos in the hope of capturing the Allied radio, but never succeeded in doing so. The guerrillas who were in charge of the radio equipment moved rapidly and easily over the rugged mountains, and whenever necessary - in the tradition of their forefathers - proved themselves invincible in combat.

Cod, how much I like
the paths of the Samaria Gorge
ever since the guerrillas walked them
during the Occupation.

Throughout the Occupation (1941-44), the Germans frequently rounded up thousands of sheep and goats on the Omalos plateau, confiscating them to feed the troops.

They also installed a petrol-driven sawmill at the spot known as *´Nero tis Perdikas´* and set about taking timber from the large pine forests nearby. This was cut into planks and floated down the river, being collected at the mouth of the stream at Ayia Roumeli. Most of the timber, however, was transported on the backs of mules confiscated from the local people.

YESTERDAY AND TODAY

The appearance of life in the gorge today bears no resemblance to what it was like before 1962. That year marked a radical change in the rhythm of life in the gorge, since it was then that the government decided to declare the area a national park - a move which was essential to protect this superb Cretan landscape.

The unfortunate aspect of the decision was that people who had been born and had lived their lives in the gorge were forced to move out. This was no small thing, if we remember that the community of the gorge had a history dating back centuries. Here, then, let us pause for a while and look at the lives of these people and the way in which they managed to survive among the rugged mountains that surrounded them.

Until 1962, the gorge contained the villages of Kato (Lower) and Pano (Upper) Samaria, whose fortunes were inextricably tied up with those of Ayia Roumeli and Omalos. The four communities formed one administrative unit, and all the inhabitants were *authentic Sphakiots*.

The harshness of life in the mountains and the wildness of the landscape are imprinted in the faces, the bodies and the characters of the Sphakiots. Genuine descendants of the Dorians, these are tall men and women with an eagle eye and lissom bodies. The women of Sphakia are noted for their beauty, which is why the folk poem urges us to go to Sphakia:

...to see the girls as pretty as pearls, with their delicate eyebrows, and there are blonde girls, too...

The Sphakiots, indomitable and unruly by nature, are also proud and self-centred. They regard themselves as a cut above the Cretans of the low-lying areas, and have little respect for the laws.

Sphakia was the place where the vendetta flourished more than anywhere else in Crete. In the Venetian period, it gained strength as more or less the only way of administering justice, since the local Venetian nobility was immune to punishment. Over the centuries, acts of vengeance acquired a veneer of respectability, and were seen as honourable and heroic. Today the custom is much less common.

The Sphakiots are much attached to their centuries-old beliefs and customs, and superstition still has great power over them; after all, their land with its caves and ravines is ideal for haunting with fairies and Nereids.

They are also pious, however, and inordinately hospitable. They are offended if a visitor to their houses cannot be treated, or will not accept the treat. There is a typical Cretan couplet about this:

*A thousand welcomes to you
my friends and relatives,
and if there's no room in my house for you
may it fall upon my head.*

The *Customs, Traditions, Feasts, Songs* and *Dances* of the Sphakiots are in line with the practices of the island in general and of western Crete in particular.

As elsewhere in Crete, the *Sphakiot wedding* is the most important of all the festivities. There is a clear distinction in Sphakiot society between those who are the offspring of *'good families'* - that is, families which turned out freedom fighters and armed band leaders - and those who are not. The children of *'good families'* would never think of looking for a marriage partner among the other part of society.

Among the traditional musical instruments which accompany the **music** of Crete, the wooden three-stringed *lyre* reigns supreme. It is played by the *lyraris*, who in turn is accompanied by the *pasadoros* with his *lagouto* (a form of lute).

One of the basic song forms is the *mantinada*, an untranslatable couplet in which each line has fifteen syllables:

A hard life and sighing
and bitterness and fear -
that is the life of the
shepherds in the plain
and up in the mountains.

The **rizitika songs**, which are not in a rhyming verse form, are the creations of a proud, free people. In former times they were only sung in western Crete, and more specifically in the upland villages in the area between the basin in the foothills ('rizes') of the White Mountains and Mt Psiloritis. Thus they acquired their name. They tell us of bravery, love, nature, hospitality and the passion for freedom:

Never weep for a brave man
even if he misses his aim,
and even if he misses once and twice
he'll still be brave
and his door will always be open...

There are links straight back to the songs about the border guards of the Byzantine Empire:

Digenes was at death's door
and the earth trembled in fear of him
and the gravestone shivered
at the thought
of covering him,
for even where he lies
he will say the words of the brave.

These mantinades and rizitika provide good examples of the Cretan dialect, which contains a rich vocabulary of its own and preserves many Byzantine words. Even the diction of the Cretans is a survival of its Doric origins.

Under Turkish rule, poetry survived thanks to the ordinary people, who preserved - deep in their memories - the works they loved best, passing them down from generation to generation in the oral tradition.

34

One example of this is the Cretan epic, a thousand lines long, composed by the shepherd Pantzalios on the subject of the rebellion of 1770, entitled *The Song of Daskaloyannis*.

The **dances** of the Cretans have a bravado that is all their own. The *'pentozalis'* is a circular dance with five *'zala'* or steps; it begins slowly and gradually builts up to a frenetic climax culminating in the leaps which are reminiscent of the Pyrrhichian war-dance of ancient Crete. The rhythmic *'syrtos'* dance, with its elaborate steps, is known here as the *'chaniotis'*.

Among the main activities of the people of this part of Crete was **stock-breeding**. Each family had its sheep and goats, whose summer pastures were at the spot known as Poria, beyond *'tou Kallergi'* (at an altitude of 1,700 metres).

Up there were makeshift *cheese dairies*, turning out the Greek version of gruyere and *'myzithra'*, a salty white cheese.

The people of Samaria and Ayia Roumeli were known as excellent **bee-keepers**, and the honey they produced was of the highest quality. Here they had the help of the vast pine forests and the incredible range of aromatic plants to be found in the vicinity, notably thyme.

For the inhabitants of the Samaria area, *cereals* were a rarity, and only the area to the north of Samaria was suitable for growing them. Each villager would have a little crop of *vegetables* in his garden, but this was only possible once fertile soil had been moved in from somewhere else.

In Omalos, on the other hand, cereals' (wheat, barley, oats, etc.) were plentiful, and the area produced renowned *potatoes*.

Sheep and goats resting in the deep shade of the tall oaks at Omalos to protect themselves from the fierce noon-day sun.

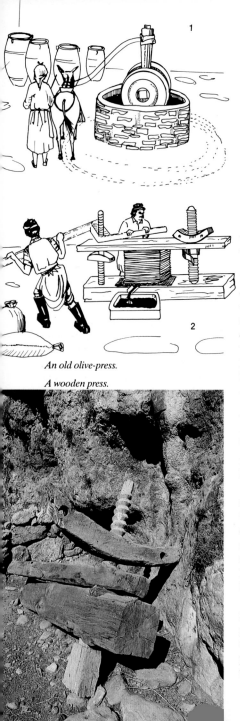

An old olive-press.

A wooden press.

Even today, there are quite a number of olive trees around Samaria for the production of olive oil. The area had *olive presses*, powered by horses or water. The olives were worked using primitive technology, and some of these early 'fabrikes' have survived down to the present day.

The village of Kato Samaria still has its primitive *wooden press* for the production of olive oil. Ano Samaria has a more modern unit, with metal presses. *The unit was worked by horse-power, which drove the horizontal millstone to crush the olives* (sketch 1). *The pulp produced by this method was then placed in sacks, which were squeezed by hand until the juice of the olives ran out. This was poured into basins and the oil removed as it separated out on the surface of the water* (sketch 2). The last of the oil produced in this way was not suitable for human consumption, and went to make *soap*.

The local people also worked as *woodcutters,* and there was a water-powered sawmill near the Iron Gates. The larger trunks were floated down the river to the sawmill or Ayia Roumeli, being towed by horses from the bank.

The power of the river waters sufficed to drive the saw that cut the trees - felled in the rich pine and cypress woods nearby - into planks and posts of all kinds. After 1945 the sawmill moved to the church of St Nicholas close to the village, where its base can still be seen today.

Among the other products of Samaria were some associated with pine trees. The bark, for instance, was useful in fishing because it floats, and pine resin was also collected for use in the making of *wine*.

Sketch of a watermill at Samaria.

Once the pine trunks (and especially the trunks of the holm oak) had been cut into sections, they were used to feed **furnaces** that turned out high-quality charcoal.

Perhaps the activity most characteristic of Samaria and the Ayia Roumeli area in particular was the district's **watermills,** of which there were ten or so. They were used for grinding wheat.

The gorge could also be used for the *fulling* of wool. The water was led through a wooden pipe or natural channel into a pool whose exit was narrowed than its entrance. The created the pressure necessary to clean (full) the skins or fleeces before they were sent off to be made into thread or wool.

Samaria had a proper *fulling-mill,* where wooden hammers beat the cloth and wool from which heavy-duty materials would be made. The cloth was placed on a horizontal axle which was turned by a mill-wheel powered by the fall of the water. The water also drove the hammers which beat the cloth on the axle, through a complex mechanism dating back to early times.

Above the village of Samaria was an area where the stones were suitable for *honing* knives, chisels and axes. The local people gathered these stones and sold them.

The collecting and selling of **dittany** and the other medicinal and aromatic plants was confined to certain families, since the first part of the process was very dangerous. Dittany, in particular, *only grows in highly inaccessible spots, in cracks in the rock which could only be reached by clambering down at the end of a rope.* For that reason, dittany-picking was usually done in teams.

37

In view of the wildness of the land in which they lived, the Sphakiots turned to the sea for a living at a very early period. Under Turkish rule, they were the only Cretans who engaged in sea trading and transport - and in piracy. The extensive forests which covered their mountains provided them with the timber they needed to build their ships. This is the place where the *mountain cypress* described by Theophrastus originated. In ancient times, timber was exported to Egypt, where it was much in demand. It was also used for the pillars of the Minoan palaces. The cypress has its place in folk poetry, too:

Slender cypress tree,
sway and raise a breeze
to make the birds sing
and dawn break.

The *wild goats* which, as we have seen, have always lived in the vicinity of Samaria were also *farmed.* They were hunted for their tasty meat and for their skins, which produced tough leather. The leather was used to make Cretan knee-boots, mats and belts. Before this, however, the hair had to be removed from it in special wooden devices called ´skales´.

Tools for working leather.

The **architecture** of the houses of the Samaria area is very simple. Their principal features are the thick walls, the medium height, the plasterwork and the arch which serves as an interior partition. In the more highly developed form of this house, the simple structure acquires a courtyard with an outdoor oven and a barn, a separate sitting-room, a kitchen and a storehouse with or without an upper floor.

The coastal type of house, as exemplified by those of Chora Sphakion, has as its main characteristic an external vault forming a kind of covered entrance porch. These stone-built houses usually have very small windows, and inside one is struck by the relative absence of furniture.

Apart from the modern houses to be seen at Omalos, the area also has a large number of older structures built in dry stone. Most of these consist of two rooms, one larger and one smaller, the latter of which serves as an ante-chamber to the former. It was also used in earlier times as accommodation for animals. In some cases, these houses have outer walls more than a metre thick. Their earthen roofs are held up by a roughly-hewn pine truck placed in the middle of the house, called the ´lyratzis´. This tree trunk supports a beam which runs the length of the house.

At the spot known as Kallergi, and also elsewhere on the Omalos plateau, are small stone structures which, from the outside, resemble nothing more than piles of stones. Inside, however, they have a false vaulted ceiling made of large stone slabs. These structures are called ´koumi´ and their purpose was to protect passing travellers from cold, snow and rain.

The tiny chapels to be seen here and there are characteristic of the area.
This is the chapel of the Sts Theodore, south-west of Omalos (see p. 51).

(see p. 51)

To the north-west of the village of Samaria, about 200 metres above the main path, are two tiny hamlets called the ´Kryptes´. These are completely invisible from the bed of the gorge and difficult to reach. Older inhabitants call them the ´Bank of Samaria´, because this is where the villagers would hide their valuables when threatened by raiding Saracens, Venetians or Turks.

The **Castles**, large and small, to be seen in the vicinity of Sphakia are evidence of the importance which the Turks attributed to being able to subjugate and control the unruly and warlike Sphakiots. They took particular care over organising the watch to be kept on the gorge and on Omalos, natural fortresses where revolutionaries from all over Crete congregated whenever a rebellion broke out.

After their victory over the Cretan rebels in 1866, at the cost of many lives, the Turks built a large number of fortresses throughout Crete. They were sited at crucial points and communicated with each other and the main castles of Chania, Rethymno and Herakleio, to give warning of possible movements on the part of the Cretans, by means of beacons - a system first established in Byzantine times.

It was impossible to approach these castles without being noticed: they were surrounded by hidden guard-posts and strongholds, many of which can still be seen today.

Most of these castles were speedily accessible - for their defenders - along two separate well-planned and carefully maintained roads, for reasons of security and to safeguard communications between different areas.

The ´Zevgospita´.

The forts were usually within sight of each other, and they had a signalling system. Very close to them were dry-stone outbuildings which were used as storerooms for wood, stables for horses and even barracks for soldiers who could not be accommodated in the main building during the course of operations.

The areas to the east and west of Ayia Roumeli each have two forts, one larger and one smaller. The role of the smaller castles was to aid the larger ones in the event of a raid. The larger forts had storerooms, fireplaces, ovens, magazines, water tanks, large halls and all the other facilities necessary to accommodate large numbers of soldiers for long periods without fresh supplies.

In 1878 the Cretans rose in rebellion once again, forcing the Turks to abandon these forts in the countryside and wall themselves up in the much larger castles at Chania, Rethymno and Herakleio.

The Ayia Roumeli area. High on the hillside we can see one of the ruined castles.

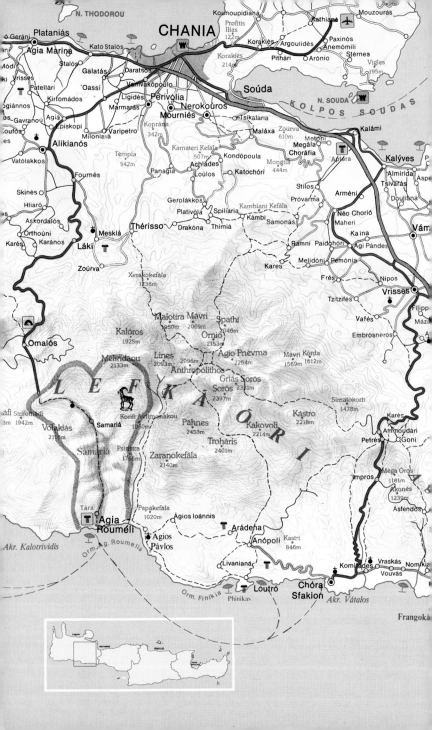

INTRODUCTION TO THE TOUR

The city of Chania is the usual starting-point for those wishing to visit the Samaria Gorge.

Chania itself can be reached:

By air to the airport at Akrotiri, 15 km. to the north-west of the city.

By sea to the enormous natural harbour at Souda, 6 km. to the east of the city.

By road from wherever else in Crete we happen to be.

We shall describe the route taken by most visitors, which is as follows:

Chania - Omalos   Page:
(by bus) 44
Omalos - Xyloskalo
(by bus) 48

THE MAIN ROUTE
(on foot)
Xyloskalo - Ayia Roumeli 56

Ayia Roumeli - Chora Sphakion
(by boat) 78
Chora Sphakion - Chania
(by bus) 80

Thie itinerary summarised above gives visitors an opportunity to see at close quarters numerous impressive animals and plants, the peculiarities of the terrain, and the human warmth of the Cretans. The variety of means of transport which have to be used and the length of the walk involved in a descent of the gorge (covering a drop in height from 1,200 metres to sea-level) will leave unforgettable memories in the mind of every visitor.

The service buses to Omalos leave Chania from the bus station to the south of the Municipal Market. The earliest bus is at 6.00 a.m. and the last is in the early evening, providing a service for those who wish to spend the night in Omalos. The frequency of the departures depends on the time of year. Buses also depart at roughly the same times for Chora Sphakion, and the service is planned so as to connect with the little boats on the Ayia Roumeli line.

Many visitors prefer to visit the gorge by means of the coaches laid on by travel agencies, which take walkers to Omalos in the morning, from all over Crete, and pick them up again in the evening from Chora Sphakion.

Those who decide to take their own cars to the top of the gorge should bear in mind that they will have to return to Omalos by bus via Chania.

Passengers are moved from Ayia Roumeli to Chora Sphakion on vessels owned by the firm set up by the people of Sphakia: one car ferry, three passenger launches and a cruise ship. The departures of these vessels vary according to the number of passengers to be moved.

Some visitors choose to stay on in Ayia Roumeli or Chora Sphakion, after walking the gorge, in order to visit the other tourist sights of southern Crete.

After describing the main walk through the gorge, we suggest some additional visits and suitable places for walking and climbing. However, this information is included largely for the purpose of giving visitors a more complete idea of the surroundings of the gorge, since most of the climbs described are difficult, require a guide and need a permit from the forestry authorities (see p. 82).

Chania - Omalos Plateau

The city of Chania stands on the site of ancient Cydonia, a powerful commercial city.

In 69 BC Cydonia was captured by the Romans, who held it until the Byzantines took over in 325 AD. In 823 it fell to the Arabs, who gave it its modern name. Under the Venetians (1252) it regained something of its former splendour and flourished as a commercial and economic centre, sometimes even being called 'the Venice of the East'.

Today, Chania is the largest city in Crete after Herakleio, with a population of 60,000. It is the commercial and administrative capital of the Prefecture by the same name. Chania consists of the **Old** and **New** Cities, which blend harmoniously into an attractive, friendly and uniform whole.

The **Old City**, with its narrow alleys and its Venetian buildings, occupies the north part of Chania and preserves a considerable part of its Venetian wall.

Aerial photograph of Chania

At the end of the sea-front towers the historic **Firka Fortress**. Here the Greek flag was raised officially for the first time in 1913, setting the seal on union with Greece. Today, the Fortress houses a **Maritime Museum**. The church of **San Francesco**, the largest Venetian church on Crete, today contains the collections of the **Archaeological Museum**.

In front of the Old City is the Venetian Harbour, with its lighthouse at the end of the pier and picturesque cafes along the quay.

The **New City**, modern and attractive, spreads out around the older quarter, with the Municipal Market as the point where the two meet. Chania is full of greenery and gardens, which is why it is sometimes called the ´*city of flowers*´.

We set out from the centre of Chania along Kissamou St, heading west. Immediately after crossing the bridge over the Kladisos river (1.5 km.) we turn left. At 3.5 km. from Chania we come to the community of Vamvakopoulo.

the usual point of departure for a visit to the gorge.

The Ayia lake, with the White Mountains in the background.

Beyond Vamvakopoulou we enter an enormous area in which olive groves alternate with orchards of orange trees. Beyond the orange groves, on the right, is the new church of Sts Constantine and Helen, beneath which is the artificial lake of **Ayia**. Water pumped out of this reservoir, and originating in a number of seemingly inexhaustible springs, irrigates the entire plain and supplies water to the surroundings of Chania.

It is to the springs that the area owes its name, which comes from the Arabic word ´aya´, meaning ´water´. The lake contains numerous species of fish and marine plant. Its waters drive a 300 KW hydroelectric generator at one end and, at the other, are led off to irrigate the greater part of the northern axis of the Prefecture of Chania.

To the left of Ayia, on a hill densely covered with pine trees, we can pick out the marble obelisk of a monument commemorating the execution of Cretan patriots by the Occupation forces. Below Ayia, to the north, is the ruinous church of Our Lady, at the foundations of which, according to tradition, a golden bell lies buried. The landscape of olives and oranges, now familiar, continues for a few more kilometres before changing abruptly at the turning for Alikianos. To the left is a two-storey monument bearing the names of the 118 Cretans executed by the Germans when they occupied this area on 1 August 1941.

A minor road branching off to the right takes us to the three-arched stone bridge over the river **Keritis** (called Iordanos in ancienttimes). Immediately beyond this we enter the village of Alikianos, 12.5 km. from Chania.

Alikianos is set among dense vegetation. It has a 14th century church of St George, in which, in 1570, the wedding was celebrated between the son of arch-rebel Georgios Kandanoleon and the daughter of the Venetian Da Molin. At the banquet which followed, the Venetians laced the wine with a potion that drugged the Cretan guests - whom they unceremoniously murdered, including the bridegroom and his father.

Leaving the monument behind us, we head south towards the village of **Fourne**, 15 km. from Chania.

A branch of the route beyond Fourne takes us to the left, and after 6 km. we come to the village of **Meskla**. The abundant water and tall plane trees which supplement the beauty of the landscape caused the ancient Cretans to be so fond of the spot that they built the ancient city of Rizenia here.

One of the tributaries of the river Keritis rises nearby, and has trout in its waters.

We return to Fourne and, leaving the turning to Meskla on our left, cross the old metal bridge over the Keritis and bid farewell to the orange groves, the last of which can be seen on our left.

Before long we cross another metal bridge over a tributary of the Keritis and begin to climb up the twisting road through dense olive groves to **Lakki** (24 km.). This village was built in Venetian times by two inhabitants of Ai-Yannis, Sphakia, and is the birthplace of Hadzimichalis Yannaris (see p. 31). The village stands on a conspicuous hill at an altitude of 500 m., with its brilliantly-white houses arranged in terraces down the slopes.

The beauty of the village was extravagently praised by the archaeologist and traveller Deffner (1918).

The struggles of the inhabitants of Lakki for their freedom from various masters were never-ending and do credit to Greek history.

The village was burned down again and again, by the Venetians, the Turks and most recently by the Germans. Quite a number of the villagers went to fight as volunteers in the Macedonian Struggle of the early 20th century.

In other words, there is hardly an inch of ground in the area around the village which has not been fought over, there is not a family which does not have its own tale of hardship and suffering, and there is not a house which does not stand on the foundations of an earlier building destroyed by some enemy or other.

After Lakki, the road begins to wind up across the rocky slopes of the White Mountains, coming after a few kilometres to a flat place at a spot known as **Fokes**.

We continue to climb, reaching the highest point on the route at ´Neratzoporos´.

A few more hairpin bends, with the ´Lakkos tou Vergeri´ on our left, bring us into sight of the Omalos plateau and we begin to descend.

Omalos - Xyloskalo

Omalos is a plateau with an area of approximately 25 square kilometres. It takes its name from the flat and smooth - that is, ´omalos´ - nature of its terrain. There are three entrances, to the north, west and south, each with its separate and independent village.

At the north entrance is the village of **Lakkiotikos Yiros** (altitude 1,050 m.), at the west entrance is the village of **Seliniotikos Yiros** (altitude 1,050 m.) and to the south is **Xyloskalo** (altitude 1,227 m.).

Apart from these three villages, various other buildings are scattered across the plain. These are uninhabited in the winter, being used only in the summer when the local people are engaged in stock-breeding, farming, bee-keeping and, of course, tourism.

The plateau is surrounded by tall mountain peaks. To the south are Gigilos (2,005 m.), Volakias 2,116 m.) and Psilafi (1,936 m.); to the west is Trouli (1,455 m.), to the north is Katrinari (1,318 m.) and to the east is Koukoules (1,640 m.). A road runs all the way round the plateau at a slightly higher level than the fields, but only the section from Lakkiotikos Yiros (at the north end) to Xyloskalo (at the south end) is surfaced.

Here, at the north end of the plateau, is the end of the old path which linked Omalos with Lakki - the legendary *Mousourou road*. The songs about this path are legion, and they tell of the fight for freedom both from foreign conquerors and from the tyrannical regimes which Greece has known from time to time.

*When will the stars shine clear
and when will spring come,
so that I can take my rifle,
my fine heirloom,*

*and go down to Omalos
to the Mousourou road
and make mothers without sons
wives without husbands...*

The *Mousourou road* was a symbol of the path towards freedom - and ever since the songs were first sung it led up to a place of liberty.

Today, the Omalos plateau is covered largely with fallow fields. Once it was used for successive crops of cereals and potatoes.

The bushes and grasses which grow there in abundance alternate in colour and flourish in the untilled soil, each in accordance with its season. In May they reach a peak of colour, vying with one another in the luxuriance of their flowers and foliage.

The hillsides round the plateau are covered with greyish-green cypresses and lighter green pines. *Phagnalon rupestre, Zelcova cretica* and mallows grow in the clearings.

It is believed that Omalos was once a lake whose waters drained out through the swallow-hole at Tzanis and emerged once more as the source of the river Keritis and at Ayia. At any rate, it has been proved that huge resources of water lie beneath the White Mountains. When the snow melts, the water permeates the limestone rock formations and, after reaching a certain level, runs off: 3/4 down the northern slopes of the White Mountains, with their many peaks, most of it reaching the Prefecture of Chania, and 1/4 in the direction of the south coast.

View of Omalos, showing the road which leads to Xyloskalo.

As the road from Chania enters the plateau at its lowest point (1,050 m.), the far end of a recess conceals the opening into the **Tzanis Cave** or **Chonos**, an enormous swallow-hole thanks to which Omalos is no longer a lake. There is a local tradition that a shepherd haunts the cave in the moonlight, playing his lyre, enchanted by the fairies.

To the right and left, on the foothills above the plateau, we can now see occasional houses. We have entered the first village of Omalos, **Lakkiotikos Yiros**, and these houses are farms or cheese dairies to some of which modern facilities have been added for the convenience of tourists. Shortly before the centre of the village, on a hill, the *tower of Hadzimichalis Yannaris* (see p. 31) stands above the other buildings, with the church of *St Pantaleimon* next to it.

The village of Lakkiotikos Yiros.

The Hadzimichalis tower with the church of St Pantaleimon, at Lakkiotikos Yiros.

Two hundred metres beyond Lakkiotikos Yiros, as we head south, we can turn right along an unsurfaced road leading south-west. Before long this will bring us to the ´Voulisma´, on our left, a depression which contains water almost all the year round and is a typical karstic phenomenon. This road continues around the plateau, linking Lakkiotikos Yiros with Seliniotikos Yiros.

On our left are successive areas of scrub and fallow fields, with wild flowers in a riot of colour, often alternating with cultivated expanses. On our right are the ´Zevgospita´, ruinous masses of boulders and occasional door or window frames to remind us of the human presence here in earlier times. These scattered structures can be seen for the next 2.5 km., after which they begin to become more frequent and gradually yield their place to more modern buildings, centred on the village in the south-west corner of the plateau, **Seliniotikos Yiros**.

If we continue from here in a south-westerly direction, we will emerge from the plateau. A climb of 1 km. brings us to the church of the **Sts Theodore**, painted white, on our left (see p. 39).

Another 8 km. of unsurfaced road will take us to the spot known as ´stis Petras to Seli´, where we join the main surfaced road from Chania to Souyia.

Two unsurfaced roads lead on from Seliniotikos Yiros to Xyloskalo. We return to the main road two hundred metres beyond Lakkiotikos Yiros. Now the holm oaks, wild pears and other trees crowd in more densely and the plateau is lost to view. On our left we pass the unsurfaced

The entrance to the Tzanis cave.

The Natural History Museum.

road that leads to the Chania Mountaineering Association's refuge at the spot known as Kallergi.

We continue south, across the glen formed by the foothills of Psilafi and the peak of Kallergi.

The road becomes narrower, and 1.5 km. before Xyloskalo we see on our right the building which houses the **Natural History Museum**, with a cafe and a souvenir shop adjacent to it.

If we now climb a little higher up (300 m.) to the attractive tourist pavilion, we will have a wonderful view from above of Xyloskalo (´wooden staircase´, south entrance to the plateau), the magnificent peak of Gigilos and a considerable section of the gorge itself. Here there is also a car park (see the photograph on pp. 52-53).

INSTRUCTIONS FOR WALKERS IN THE GORGE

(from the sign before Xyloskalo)

MINISTRY OF AGRICULTURE: DIRECTORATE OF FORESTS AND THE FOREST ENVIRONMENT
SAMARIA NATIONAL PARK
(WHITE MOUNTAINS, CRETE)
OPERATING REGULATIONS OF THE NATIONAL PARK
OPENING DATES AND HOURS

THE SAMARIA NATIONAL PARK IS OPEN TO VISITORS FROM 1 MAY TO 31 OCTOBER EACH YEAR, FROM 6 A.M. TO 3 P.M. EVERY DAY. BETWEEN 3 P.M. AND SUNSET VISITORS WILL BE ADMITTED ONLY TO THE FIRST TWO KILOMETRES OF THE PATH FROM EACH OF THE ENTRANCES (XYLOSKALO AND AYIA ROUMELI).

— INSTRUCTIONS FOR VISITORS —

VISITORS MAY WALK ONLY ALONG THE MAIN PATH (SIGNPOSTED) FROM XYLOSKALO TO AYIA ROUMELI AND VICE VERSA. THOSE WISHING TO WALK ALONG ANY OF THE OTHER PATHS MUST HAVE WRITTEN PERMISSION FROM THE CHANIA DIRECTORATE OF FORESTS AND WILL BE SUBJECT TO STRICT CHECKS.

— THE FOLLOWING ACTIVITIES ARE STRICTLY PROHIBITED —

LIGHTING FIRES. CAMPING. OVERNIGHT STAYS IN THE NATIONAL PARK. PICKING FLOWERS. UPROOTING OR DESTROYING PLANTS. THE REMOVAL OR DESTRUCTION OF NESTS, EGGS AND FLEDGLINGS. DESTRUCTION OR DAMAGE TO GEOLOGICAL FORMATIONS, SIGNS AND OTHER PROPERTY OF THE NATIONAL PARK, AND CULTURAL MONUMENTS. POSSESSION OF WEAPONS OR TRAPS. DOGS. HUNTING AND FISHING IN THE PARK. SWIMMING IN THE STREAMS.

— THE FOLLOWING ACTIVITIES ARE NOT PERMITTED —

RADIOS. SINGING. THROWING STONES. EXCESSIVE NOISE. THE DISPOSAL OF RUBBISH IN PLACES OTHER THAN THOSE PROVIDED. SMOKING ANYWHERE OTHER THAN THE REST POINTS. THE CONSUMPTION OF ALCOHOL.

— PROTECTIVE MEASURES —

THE NATIONAL PARK IS PATROLLED BY FORESTRY SERVICE RANGERS BASED AT FOUR POINTS INSIDE THE PARK: NEROUTSIKO, RIZA SYKIAS, AYIOS NIKOLAOS AND METAMORFOSI. THERE ARE FIRE POINTS WITH FIRE-EXTINGUISHING EQUIPMENT AND FIRST AID KITS. THIS EQUIPMENT AND THE CONTENTS OF THE FIRST AID KITS ARE TO BE USED BY VISITORS IN THE EVENT OF FIRE OR ACCIDENT AND ARE NOT TO BE DAMAGED. THE VILLAGE OF SAMARIA HAS A TELEPHONE FOR COMMUNICATION WITH THE POLICE, A PHARMACY, A HELIPORT AND TWO MULES TO TRANSPORT INJURED PERSONS.

— CONSEQUENCES OF FAILURE TO COMPLY WITH THE ABOVE —

THOSE WHO VIOLATE THE REGULATIONS WILL BE PROSECUTED AND PUNISHED IN ACCORDANCE WITH ARTICLES 268, 275, 276, 277, 280, 281, 283, 285, 286 AND 287 OF LEGISLATIVE DECREE 86/1969 'CONCERNING THE FORESTRY CODE' AND THE PROVISIONS OF LEGISLATIVE DECREE 996/71. THE RANGERS AND THE STAFF OF THE NATIONAL PARK SHALL BE COMPETENT TO ENFORCE THE ABOVE.

CHANIA DIRECTORATE OF FORESTS
tel. no. 22 287

*Entrance to the gorge is free for children aged up to 15,
the handicapped and organised groups of students and schoolchildren
with the written permission of the Forestry Service.*

WALKING THE GORGE

MAIN ROUTE
Xyloskalo - Ayia Roumeli (16.7 km.)
Walking time: approximately 6 hrs.

A visit to Xyloskalo, by bus or private car, is a possibility for anyone on holiday in Crete. No particular preparation is necessary and return is made by the same route.

However, those who wish to walk the Samaria Gorge and to make the most of that unique experience will have to be prepared for 5-6 hours walking and return by a different route (see the introduction to the tour, p. 43).

Walkers must be equipped with suitable stout shoes or boots and a certain amount of food. Water will not be necessary, as there are streams and springs with good, clean water all along the gorge.

The gorge starts at the Xyloskalo, at an altitude of 1,200 metres, and ends at Ayia Roumeli, on the coast. It separates the main bulk of the White Mountains, to the east, from Mt Volakias to the west. The unique view of the seemingly bottomless ravine is of unparalleled majesty.

Before starting down the gorge, please read once more the National Park regulations on p. 54.

XYLOSKALO

Legend

—·—·— National par[k]

▪▪▪▪▪ Central Rou[te]

🕆 Archaeologi[cal]

🔺 Gave

🏰 Castle

🕂 Church

⚓ Anchorage

☂ Beach

THE MAIN ROUTE		
Section	**Length**	**Time**
	(in km.)	(in min.)
Xyloskalo-Neroutsiko	1.70	45
Neroutsiko-Riza Sykias	1.00	20
Riza Sykias - Ayios Nikolaos	1.00	20
Ayios Nikolaos - Vrysi	0.80	15
Vrysi - Samaria	2.90	60
Samaria - Nero tis Perdikas	1.00	20
Nero tis Perdikas - Kefalovrysia	2.90	45
Kefalovrysia - church of Christ	1.00	20
Church of Christ - Iron Gates	0.60	15
Iron Gates - Forestry Post	1.40	30
Forestry Post - Ayia Roumeli	2.40	45
Total	**16.70**	**6 hours**

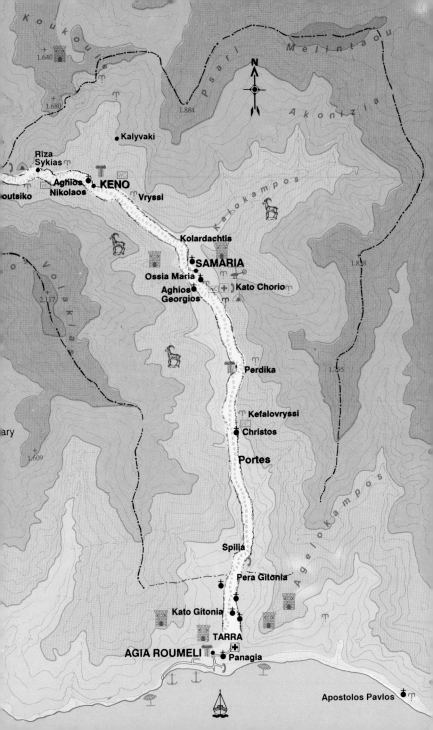

Xyloskalo, the ´wooden staircase´, is located at a distance of 45 km. from Chania and can be reached by service bus. When it became very difficult to reach the Omalos plateau from the Samaria Gorge, the local people built a kind of staircase out of pieces of wood and tree-trunks nailed to the rocks so that they could cross the ravine. This is the wooden staircase from which Xyloskalo takes its name. There is a myth about a shepherd who makes music in a cave near Xyloskalo, while fairies sing mournfully.

Today, Xyloskalo has a large wooden parapet to protect visitors and there are stone slabs to make the descent easier. We return to the car park to make our final preparations, and then begin the walk down the Samaria Gorge. Now we are at a height of 1,200 metres above sea level, and the air is chilly in the morning or evening. Enchanted by the superb landscape with the peak of Mt Gigilos and the deep ravine at our feet, we begin the descent.

After a few stone steps we pass the Forestry Service post and the path begins to wind back and forth. The further we descend, the more majestic the landscape becomes. Wild nature can be seen here in all its magnificence, and we experience feelings of admiration blended with awe in the face of such unearthly beauty. Our steps on the stone pathway seem to become lighter.

The Neroutsiko spring.

The Riza Sykias spring.

Our gaze loses itself in the dense foliage of the aged cypresses and pine trees; when it breaks free of their spell, it climbs to the steep and silvery peak of Mt Gigilos and the distant summits of the White Mountains. The primitive beauty of the gorge alternates with all kinds of other impressions which vie with one another to imprint themselves first upon our memory. But now the first three quarters of an hour have passed, and without realising it we have come to **Neroutsiko**, the first shady spring along our route.

After drinking at the stone fountain, we continue downhill. A few metres away from the path on a left-hand bend are wooden benches on which we may rest, shaded by tall and ancient pines. As we descend, the gradient gradually becomes less pronounced. A pebbly stream-bed keeps company with us on the right, and in places the path actually goes down into its bottom of round boulders.

After two or three more crossings of the stream we come to the next spring, **Riza Sykias**, on our left. Twenty or thirty minutes later we come to the first stream of water rising on the north flank of the route. This stream once powered a sawmill whose foundations have survived. The gorge begins to widen out and a further ten minutes bring us to the centre of a flat spot - **Ayios Nikolaos**.

The chapel of St Nicholas, surrounded by huge cypresses.

The chapel of St George.

The simple church of **St Nicholas,** from which this place takes its name, stands in a location of exotic beauty where there is also a stone Forestry Service guardpost and an attractive fountain beneath a proud cypress tree. In was on this divine site that the ancient Cretans built the city of Caeno, where the goddess Britomartis was born (see p. 22). As we continue to the south-east, the beautiful natural platform begins to narrow and the trees close in. Within quarter of an hour we are at the next attractive stone-built fountain, **Vrysi**.

The spring at Vrysi.

During the course of the walk we will have to cross the river many times, seeing the surrounding mountain peaks and the foliage of the trees reflected in its clear waters. Soon we leave the river-bed on our left, however, and the path climbs. From this point we begin to see the Kalokambos ravine, with the peaks of Psaris and Melindaou which enclose it. To the right of Kalokambos, on a hilltop, are the ruins of a Turkish tower. Now the path runs downhill again, zigzagging back to the river-bed. This area is known as **Kolardachtis** and there are many strongholds from Turkish times in the vicinity.

In front of us, to the south, towers the hill on which stands the church of **St George**, with an ancient cypress tree whose trunk is wedged in between two rocks.

Descending the 'Kolardachtis'.

Shortly before Samaria.

The village of Pano Samaria, once bustling with life.

The bridge leading to the ruinous village of Samaria.

The village of Pano Samaria.

The Forestry Service guardpost.

A hundred metres on, after a sharp right-hand turn, we get our first view of the village of **Pano Samaria**. We follow the path, which can only just be seen on the river-bed and then runs on its right bank, and pass below the hill on which, out of sight, stands the pretty church of *St George*. At the foot of the hill, next to the path, are numerous olive trees planted by the villagers in earlier times.

The river-bed becomes deeper here, and to visit the village we must leave the path, to the left, and cross a concrete bridge which spans the river, resting on an earlier bridge consisting of two huge cypress trunks. The square of the old village opens out immediately across the bridge. It is surrounded by two restored buildings and a number of ruinous structures.

There are also quite a few mulberry trees, under one of which the Forestry Service has built a stone fountain whose water never stops running. In the courtyard of the Forestry Service guardpost is a second fountain, and both together quench the thirst of hot walkers.

We return to the path and, leaving the bridge on our left, continue in a southerly direction. After just a few steps there is a narrow passage between the river bank and a large steep-sided rock.

This narrow opening contains a number of ruinous buildings which are reminiscent of a fortified post to control the pass. After this, on our right in a hollow in the rock, is a tiny *church of Christ*.

All that has remained of the living-rooms and vaulted basements of Kato Samaria.

Further along, on the left, is the makeshift heliport which is used for moving injured visitors out of the gorge. We turn left and from the edge of the heliport descend into the stream-bed. On the other side, on a small flat space, are the ruinous buildings of the village of **Kato Samaria**. A walk along the overgrown stone paths through the ruins will reveal to us the old living-rooms and vaulted basements of houses which once bustled with life.

Today, only wild figs and other semi-wild trees inhabit the village. We leave Kato Samaria behind and climb in a north-easterly direction, soon coming to the little church of **the Blessed Mary**, surrounded by cypress trees.

Close to the church is a cave in which the Blessed Mary, a woman of Egypt, lived as a hermit. **Samaria** is a corruption of her name: Osia Maria - Sia Maria - Samaria.

We return to the main path and leave the heliport on our left, continuing south. A well-maintained path runs parallel to the river-bed, at a somewhat higher level. In among the pines and cypresses which are characteristic of the area are numerous olive trees, which once met the local people's needs in olive oil. We then cross to the east bank of the river over a little bridge.

The little bridge beyond Samaria which affords access to the east bank of the river.

Less than 20 minutes' walk from the village, we come to the next stone-built fountain, at the spot called *'tis Perdikas to nero'*. A little further on, almost in the bed of the river - which gradually begins to narrow, with the area occupied by water spreading out towards the walls - we can see the base of the engine-powered sawmill which once operated here. A few more minutes bring us down into the stony bed of the river, and the walls of the gorge, now vertical, tower hundreds of metres above us.

This is the beginning of the section of the gorge known as the *Iron Gates* from its narrowness. The path often disappears entirely as it meanders in and out among the boulders, of all sizes, with which the stream-bed is littered.

The endless cliffs which line the route, now closer to us and now farther away, follow the winding path of the stream.

The path now crosses to the left bank, and at the spot known as *'Halasmena Gremna'* or *'tou Sarakinou i Pate'* the ground is liable to subsidence. In the 1920s there were extensive landslides here, as a result of which a lake of water was formed. Our descent of the gorge is accompanied by the soughing of the pines in the breeze.

After 45 minutes' walk from To Nero tis Perdikas we come to the spot known as *Kefalovrysia*, shaded by plane trees. The ancient water-loving trees cover the river-bed from side to side.

Abundant springs of ice-cold water well up from the roots of these trees. According to archaeologists, they once supplied the oracle which was located somewhere in the vicinity. Nowadays the water is led off in pipes to supply the village of Ayia Roumeli.

Shortly after Kefalovrysia we rejoin, on our left, the path which we left behind before the springs. It has been cut out of the left bank of the river, above the water which runs all the year round at this point.

To the right, as we walk down the path, is the water channel of the old watermill which once stood here, with traces of the buildings. Nearby, on the right, is a stone water fountain. As we follow the path south, the gorge begins to narrow again and the vertical walls draw closer together. The path crosses and re-crosses the river, and narrow places come rapidly one after another.

Fifteen minutes' walk from the church of Christ bring us to the *Iron Gates,* as they are known locally and internationally. Here the spectacle is overwhelming, as the walls of the gorge approach so close to each other that one has the impression they are going to bar one's way completely. At the Gates, they are only 3 metres apart and rise to 700 metres on either side.

These perpendicular rocky walls, with the pines and holm oaks which grow in their cracks and the water of the stream passing between them, are the most magnificent and imposing part of the walk.

The wildness of the terrain and the inaccessible steep cliffs which create a feeling of awe are the reason why the Cretan wild goat (see p. 15) has managed to survive in the area.

If we were to pass through the Gates at dawn or during the night, we would be in danger of being hit by the falling stones knocked down by the wild goats as they scramble about high on the cliffs in search of food. Stones may also be dislodged by the sharp change in temperature from day to night. It is easy to imagine the deafening noise of falling rocks, shattering into smaller pieces, as a kind of wild music.

The passage through the Gates is very dangerous in the evening and throughout the winter months. This is why it is only permitted to walk the gorge during specific hours of the day and at specific times of the year.

The Iron Gates have become a symbol of the Prefecture of Chania and of Crete as a whole.

Refreshments and souvenirs are on sale at 'Spilia'.

After the Gates, the gorge widens out again. After half an hour's walk, we come to the Forestry Service guardpost, on the right of the rocky stream-bed, which marks the end of the gorge proper. After the guardpost the path continues along the right bank of what is now a broad valley, and we come to the village of **Ayia Roumeli**.

According to Papagrigorakis, the name of the village comes from the Arab root *'aya'*=water, and *'rumeli'*=Greek - i.e., *'Greek water'*. Deffner adds that the name of the nearby temple may have had its part to play, too, through confusion with the Roman goddess Rumilia who is mentioned by Plutarch.

We come first to **Spilia**, one of the several 'quarters' of which the Community of Ayia Roumeli consists. Here there are shops selling refreshments and souvenirs.

Spilia, with its few houses, is succeeded by **Mesoyeitonia**, which is larger and has a little cafe.

We leave Mesoyeitonia and proceed with the river-bed on our left, soon coming to **Kato Yeitonia**, the last part of the village on the west bank. There are quite a number of houses here, many of them ruined, and a church of *St George*. Near the last houses of Kato Yeitonia we cross an arched bridge over the stream and find ourselves almost inside the precinct of the church of the *Holy Trinity*.

The church of the Holy Trinity.

To the east of the Holy Trinity, close at hand, is a district consisting of ruinous houses known as **Pera Yeitonia**. We leave the Holy Trinity behind and walk along the path down the centre of the valley.

The further we proceed, the lower the hills become and the more we can see of the sea. We cross the river-bed one more time and, after walking along the right bank at the foot of the hill which forms a partial barrier into the valley, we see on our right the first houses in the coastal part of the village of Ayia Roumeli. To the left, after the broad mouth of the river, is the sea. Also on our left, in the river-bed, is an arched bridge which is no longer in use. A Turkish tower is visible on top of the hill.

To our left is the water channel for one of the 15 watermills which used to operate in the stretch of the gorge from the Gates to the sea.

Further down, on the right, we can see the church of *Our Lady*, built on the foundations of an ancient temple to Apollo or Britomartis. The buildings around this temple are the only visible remains of the ancient city of Tarra which visitors can see today (see p. 26).

The houses in the village now become more frequent. Restaurants and tourist shops line the street as we head down to the main harbour, washed by the clear blue waters of the Libyan Sea. At the end of the beach is a second, smaller, harbour, beyond which rise the steep cliffs which are typical of the coast of southern Crete.

The church of Our Lady, and a detail from its mosaics.
The main harbour of Ayia Roumeli, on the Libyan Sea.

Ayia Roumeli - Loutro-Chora Sphakion

The route from Ayia Roumeli to Chora Sphakion is that taken by most of the visitors to the gorge. Travelling east, the boat trip to Loutro takes 45 minutes and to Chora Sphakion 1 hour.

This is a very pleasant trip along the south coast of Crete. After leaving Ayia Roumeli, the first sight of interest is the Byzantine chapel of *St Paul* and the pine-clad slopes of the White Mountains, which run down to the sea. Their bare peaks, above the steep cliffs, seem to be hovering in mid-air.

Before coming to a short, low promontory, we will see the mouth of

The little church of St Paul, to the east of Ayia Roumeli.

Ayia Roumeli, the only way into or out of the gorge to the south.

the **Aradaina** gorge, whose high walls reach the sea.

Lower down, on the coast, are the few buildings of **Phinikas**, mostly intended for the use of tourists. On the low promontory is a large Turkish tower, whose bulk dominates the area. As soon as we round the cape we see the attractive and picturesque village of **Loutro** (see p. 90).

We continue east on the ship, with the steep coastline characteristic of the route on our left.

At about halfway to Chora Sphakion we come to the pretty beach of **Glyka Nera**, covered with tiny pebbles. Visitors often camp here to enjoy the beauties of the spot, sometimes for several days.

The mouth of the Aradaina gorge.

Attractive Loutro can only be reached from the sea.

Now we can see **Chora Sphakion** in front of us, and before long we disembark in its bustling and pretty harbour.

The village, which is the principal settlement in the Province of Sphakia, rises above us nestling into the bottom of a cliff. Its houses, placed one above the other, make the most of a naturally amphitheatrical site to enjoy superb views out to the Libyan Sea.

The landscape is wild, harsh and imposing, dominated as it is by the White Mountains - or ´Sphakianes Madares´, as they are known locally. The entire area is full of ravines, gorges, difficult passes and remote mountain peaks. Even the name conveys this: Sphakia comes from the word ´sphax´, meaning a chasm in the ground, so this is the ´Land of Ravines´. Thanks to its position and the bravery of its inhabitants, Sphakia was never enslaved and was a focus for revolutions and bloody battles.

Communications between Sphakia and the rest of Crete are by road, while small boats sail along the southern coast and out to the islet of Gavdos.

Chora Sphakion - Chania

From Chora Sphakion we return directly to Chania: there are service buses which connect with the arrivals of boats from Ayia Roumeli.

The road to Chania leaves Sphakia to the north. Shortly after the village of Komitades the road narrows and begins to zigzag upwards, passing through the **Imvros gorge**. This ravine is 6-7 km. in length and has high, steep sides. The itinerary is an impressive one, with pines, cypresses and holm oaks in the background and up the slopes of the mountains, and the Libyan Sea behind us. We

The Sphakiots stand out for their traditional costumes and fine physique.

complete our parallel route through the gorge when we come to the attractive little village of **Imvros**.

We now continue across the fertile **Askyfou plateau**. Shortly before the exit from the plateau is the historic village of **Askyfou**.

Now we enter another, shorter, ravine, only 2 km. in length - the ´Langos tou Katre´. Next comes the **Krapi valley**, a deep green sea of wild olives and holm oaks, which serves as a natural boundary between the Provinces of Sphakia and Apokoronou.

At 33 km. we come to **Vryses**, a most attractive village on the banks of the river Vrysanos. There are shady plane trees and numerous streams.

After Vryses, the road turns north and west and we return to Chania. *This is the end of the classic circular route by which we visit the Samaria Gorge.*

GETTING TO KNOW THE AREA ROUND THE GORGE
Brief boat or car trips - Walks - Climbs

Xyloskalo - Gigilos

We take the path that heads upwards in a south-westerly direction from Xyloskalo. At the first turn to the left is a ruined Turkish tower, and there are views of the Samaria Gorge, the peak of Mt Gigilos and, to the right, the Omalos plateau.

After we have been climbing for an hour the path comes to an end. Omalos is now lost to sight behind us, and we cross the wire fence which marks the edge of the National Park and begin to descend. The cliffs of crumbling rock on our right, which continue to the left, keep our hearts in our mouths as our route lies through them.

At one sharp right-hand bend the path disappears for a moment, but we shall have no difficulty finding it again as it passes through a rock with a hole in it, the *Xepitiras Cave* (see photograph on p. 6), as it is called, in the area known as Krevatsoula. The trunks of the old maple trees and cypresses begin to thin out, giving place to large rock masses in various shapes which make the whole area look particularly wild.

Below, to the left, at quite a distance from the Xepitiras Cave, is the inaccessible Daimonospilio Cave (see p. 22).

The cliffs of Mt Gigilos are very close at hand now, and after passing around the feet of the last towering rocks we suddenly see the Anoseli spring in front of us. To the right are the precipices of the Galati summit.

So far the walk has taken us two hours, and we are at an altitude of 1,500 m. After refreshing ourselves with the blessed ice-cold waters of the spring, we continue our climb. In just a few metres the precipices of Gigilos begin on our left.

As we climb, the ground becomes firmer. After a climb of 45 minutes, we find ourselves on the *Gigilos saddle*, the ´Seli Gigilou´. To the south we can see the beginning of the *Tripiti gorge* and part of its course, and in the distance is the Libyan Sea with the islets of Gavdos and Gavdopoula.

We now follow the route marked with red crosses to the west and begin to climb Mt Gigilos. After 15 minutes we come, on the right, to the mouth of a pothole which speleologists have explored to a depth of 120 metres.

An hour's climb from the Gigilos saddle will suffice to bring us to the summit, at an altitude of 2,008 metres. From the peak of Gigilos we can see Chania and the north coast as far as Kolimbari, the entire Omalos plateau with Xyloskalo, and the Samaria Gorge, which begins 1,000 metres below us at the bottom of a sheer drop.

To the north-east we can see the Mountaineering Association shelter at Kallergi, the peaks of Psaris and Melindaou, and to the right almost all the summits of the White Mountains, of which Pachnes is the tallest. Very much closer, to the north-east, is the summit of Volakias and the Tripiti gorge, while the peak of Psilafi can be seen to the west.

Seli Gigilou - Volakias

A path leads down to the south-east from the Gigilos saddle. To the left is the peak of Gigilos, and straight ahead is Mt Volakias. After crossing the saddle, we climb to the summit of **Mt Volakias** (2,117 m.), in approximately 1 1/2 hours.

To the north and north-east we can see Xyloskalo, the peak and shelter of Kallergi, and the area around the villages of Samaria.

In the distance we can distinguish Pachnes and most of the summits of the White Mountains. To the south is the mouth of the Klados gorge and the Tripiti gorge, and to the north-west towers the bulk of Gigilos and Mt Psilafi.

Seli Gigilou - Achlada - Koustoyerako

If we head south-west from the Gigilos saddle, without losing height, two hours' walk will bring us to **Achlada**, at an altitude of 1,700 metres. Here there are a number of old, ruinous cheese dairies and a tank which contains drinkable water.

We head south along a well-maintained path which runs parallel to the bed of a seasonal river for most of its length. This will take us from Achlada to the village of **Koustoyerako** in about 3 1/2 hours.

The walk takes us through a densely-vegatated area of particular interest for its natural beauty.

Crumbling rock in the vicinity of the gorge.

Omalos - Kallergi

1.5 km. before we reach Xyloskalo along the road from Lakkiotikos Yiros, we turn east up an unsurfaced road in the direction of the peak of Mt Kallergi (5 km.), at 1,750 metres, where the Chania Mountaineering Association has a shelter.

From Kallergi we can see a considerable part of the Samaria Gorge and the peaks, among others, of Mts Gigilos, Volakias and Pachnes. This is a very easy walk and can be covered in an hour and a quarter.

Kallergi - Pachnes

From Kallergi one can climb to the summit of Mt Pachnes, the highest peak in the White Mountains at 2,453 metres. The walk takes 16 hours.

Kallergi - Poria - Psaris - Melindaou

The unsurfaced motor road continues from Kallergi to the spot known as Poria, a distance which can be covered on foot in 1 1/4 hours.

From Poria we can climb to the summits of Mt Psaris (1,884 m.) in 2 hours and then continue to the peak of Melindaou (2,134 m.) in 3 hours.

Omalos - Psilafi

Mt Psilafi rises to the south-west of the Omalos Plateau, and stands 1,984 metres high.

From its peak almost all of western Crete is visible. The easiest route to the summit is along the bed of the Xeropotamos river, to the south of Omalos (2 1/2 hours).

View of Omalos.

Xyloskalo - Klados Gorge

The Klados or Domaton Gorge is shorter than the Samaria Gorge but, if anything, is even more imposing. *It is even wilder, and is inaccessible without a guide.* The walk from Omalos to the mouth of the gorge on the Libyan Sea takes at least 13 hours.

The route through the gorge starts at Xyloskalo and follows this itinerary: Linoseli - Seli Gigilou - Mitato Tzatzimou (clear path) - Psyristra - Mamounoyiorgi - Halases - Armi Kantili - Moni - Pato Kokkinovari - Nero Flokos (rudimentary path only, do not attempt without the help of a guide).

After Nero Flokos the walk continues through a trackless area where the rock is crumbly and there are dangerous cliffs and passes. After Floko we reach the bottom of the gorge at the spot called Mavri Thalassa.

This is the site of the Kastelliana heights, after which we walk down the river bed until we reach the sea. The gorge itself is a deep karstic phenomenon with a depth of some 800 metres. Mt Kokkinovari, which has been sliced away by erosion, slopes down to the bottom of the gorge.

The Kastelliana heights are perpendicular rocks which stand in the river bed and have a height of 150 metres. Their tops are covered with dense growths of pine. In some places, the route narrows to barely 1.5 metres, and the sunlight never reaches the bottom of the gorge. In the surrounding area are dense pine and cypress forests. Wild goats are frequent, and there are even some pairs of lammergeiers, which only nest here.

Ayia Roumeli can be reached after five hours' difficult walk by heading east at the mouth of the gorge. To the west, two hours' walk brings us to the mouth of the Tripiti gorge and a further five hours will be needed to reach the village of **Souyia**.

Xyloskalo - Tripiti Gorge

The Tripiti gorge is to the west of the Samaria and Domaton Gorges. It has numerous precipitous cliffs. There are difficult places, too, and the gorge should not be attempted without a guide. The landscape is very wild, and the path to the south exit often disappears.

The total length of the walk along the route from Xyloskalo to the sea via Linoseli - Seli Gigilou - Kouroupitou - Sellakia - Patos - Tripiti is 8 hours, to which 5 and 7 hours, respectively, have to be added for the walk from the mouth of the gorge to Ayia Roumeli or Souyia. The gorge is full of dense pine, cypress and maple woods, and there are only a few springs of water. The spot in the gorge known as *Lourous* has the tallest and most impressive cypresses in the entire White Mountains. Domesticated sheep and goats graze in the gorge, and the wild goat breeds freely. This is also the place where dittany is easiest to find, though at considerable distances from the sea. The entire area of the gorge is privately-owned land.

Ayia Roumeli - Souyia

To the west of Ayia Roumeli is the coastal village of **Souyia**. There is a path from one village to another, but it is difficult to find and passes through some wild, hard places. The route lies at some distance inland, so as to avoid the sharp rises and falls of the coastal cliffs. *Visitors are not recommended to take this route without a guide.* There are only a few springs of water, and they are well-hidden. For those who know the area, the walk takes 12 hours, and it is a route of incredible beauty, with steep cliffs, sandy beaches, forests and gorges among its attractions.

Souyia is easy to reach from Ayia Roumeli by boat. Even further to the west, we can travel on to Palaiochora and Elafonisi.

Ayia Roumeli - Elygia Gorge

The Elygia gorge lies to the east of Samaria, opening on to the Libyan Sea. The area has a large population of wild goats and all the species in the fauna of the White Mountains will be found there. The mountains which tower to the right and left of the dry river-bed are clothed in thick forests of pine and cypress. There are only a few well-hidden springs of water: so few, in fact, that the gorge could be described as waterless.

This gorge, too, is such a wild place that it should only be attempted with a guide. As is the case with all the gorges in the area, the densely-wooded walls often draw so close together as to form ´gates´.

A tower at Angelokambi.

Approximately halfway along the gorge is a spot called *Fliskounia*, where there is a flat area of about one hectare. Rainwater gathers here and the accumulated earth has encouraged the growth of trees which are taller than almost anywhere else (cypresses, pines, fig-trees, wild pears, etc.).

The mouth of the gorge is much broader than its course, and it plunges steeply down behind the long beach at Ayia Roumeli.

The walk from the mouth of the gorge on the Libyan Sea to the spot known as Potamos takes at least 7 hours and a guide is essential. The gorge can also be reached from Omalos and the village of Ayios Ioannis.

Souyia, to the west of Ayia Roumeli, with its long pebbly beach.

Ayia Roumeli - Angelokambi

The peak to the east of the mouth of the Samaria Gorge is known as *Angelokambi*. On it stand two Turkish towers, close together, of which the more northerly is the larger. To the south and west of this spot are steep and inaccessible precipices.

The towers stand at an altitude of 600 metres, and from them the bay of Ayia Roumeli and all the old parts of the village are visible, as are the Iron Gates of the Samaria Gorge and many of the peaks in the White Mountains, in the other direction. The easiest way up to this viewpoint is from the Elygia gorge. Half an hour from the mouth of the gorge is a sheep-fold under a rock, on our left. To the left of the fold is a path leading up to the towers. The walk takes four hours from Ayia Roumeli. Water is scarce.

The ruined lighthouse on Gavdos.

Ayia Roumeli - Gavdos

From Ayia Roumeli, we can take the boat out to the islet of Gavdos: the trip takes about three hours. This is the most southerly inhabited place in Europe, lying 28 nautical miles from Crete and about 150 from the coast of Africa. The island has a surface area of only 37 square kilometres. It is almost entirely covered with pine trees and cedars.

Gavdos has numerous sandy beaches and points of archaeological interest, but the facilities for tourists are not as highly developed as elsewhere in Crete. The most popular places with visitors are Karaves (where there is a little harbour) and the beaches of Ayios Yeorgios and Sarakiniko.

According to some scholars, this was Ogygia, the island of Calypso where Odysseus was shipwrecked in Homer's epic.

Gavdos can also be visited from Chora Sphakion.

Ayia Roumeli - Ayios Pavlos - Loutro - Chora Sphakion

We head east from Ayia Roumeli along the beach. After crossing the broad river-bed (dry in the summer months) we follow the coastline and the sandy path, which sometimes runs along the shore and sometimes winds through the rocks behind the beach. An hour and a half will bring us to the mouth of the Elygia gorge. Now the coastline becomes more precipitous and the path is on a ledge a little higher up. It gradually descends, and in a further half-hour we come to the pretty Byzantine church of *St Paul*, next to the sea.

Shortly after the church the path turns inland and does not return to the sea again until we come to the mouth of the *Aradaina* gorge (see p. 93). The route then takes us through Phinikas and Loutro and takes a total of five hours. Springs of water are few and far between, and tree cover is scanty or non-existent for most of the way.

Loutro is an attractive little coastal village which stands on the site of ancient *Phoenicas* (Katopolis). It is normally accessible only by sea.

However, there is a good path from Loutro to Chora Sphakion, which can be reached in two hours' walk.

*The Byzantine chapel of St Paul,
on the way to Loutro.*

The pretty harbour of Chora Sphakion. On the right, the road to Anopoli.

Sphakia - Anopoli (12 km.)

A road climbs out of Sphakia to the north-west and snakes up to **Anopoli** along a route with superb views of the Libyan Sea and the surrounding mountains. The village stands on a small but fertile plateau, on the site of an ancient city by the same name. The rebel Daskaloyannis, who envisaged an independent Crete, was born in Anopoli (see p. 30).

There were two cities in the vicinity in antiquity: Anopolis and Katopolis, on the site of modern Loutro and better known as Phoenicas.

Between the Anopoli plateau and that of Aradaina is the stunning **Aradaina gorge**. *An awe-inspiring metal bridge links the two plateaus.*

Sphakia - Frangokastelo

We head north from Sphakia, and then turn right for the village of Komitades. The road continues to the east, leading to the *historical castle of Frangokastelo*, on the coast. This Venetian fortress stands on the edge of a vast bare plain, and has survived in good condition. It is laid out as a square, with a tower at each corner. A plaque with the lion of St Mark in relief can be seen above the gate, between the Quirini and Dolfin crowns. The history of the castle is bound up with some of the fiercest battle of the Cretan people.

Frangokastelo from the sea.

Index

A
Achlada 84
Adrasteia nymph 18
Aegeis.................................10
Agrimi 15,19
Alikianos 47
Amaltheia 18
Ambelitsa 12
Aradaina 79
Artemis...............................28
Askyfou 80
Ayia lake 46
Ayia Roumeli 7,74,76
Ayios Nikolaos 60,63

B
Bee-Keeper.......................35
Blessed Mary 27,68
Britomartis........................18

C
Caeno 22
Castles 39
Chania 44,45
Chicory 14
Chora Sfakion.............80,92
Chrysomalousa 27
Church of Christ...............72
Church of Our Lady 76

D
Daimonospilio 22,82
Dances...............................35
Daskaloyannis...................30
Diktyna 22
Dittany........................13,37

E
Elygia Gorge.....................88
Erontas 13

F
Fliskounia 89
Fokes 47
Fourne 47
Frangokastelo...................93

G
Gavdos...............................89
Glyka Nera........................79
Gigilos 20,51,82

Golden eagle.....................15
Gypaetus 15
Gyps...................................15

H
Hadzimichalis 31,50
Holy Trinity 74
Homer 19

I
Ide nymph 18
Imvros gorge 80
Iron Gates 7,72

K
Kallergi 51,86
Kato Samaria....................68
Kato Yeitonia 74
Kefalovrysia 69
Keritis river 47
Klados Gorge....................87
Kolardachtis......................63
Koumi................................38
Koustoyerako 84
Krapi valley 80

L
Lakki.................................47
Lakkiotikos Yiros.............48
Loutro.........................79,90

M
Mallow...............................14
Mantinada.........................34
Melindaou 86
Meskla 47
Mesoyeitonia 74
Mousourou road 48

N
Natural History Museum..51
Neratzoporos 47
Neroutsiko 60

O
Olive presses 36
Omalos 48

P
Pachnes 7,86

Pano Samaria....................65
Partridges 15
Pera Yeitonia....................74
Phinikas.............................79

R
Riza Sykias........................60
Rizitika 34
Poria 86
Potamou Gorge................87
Psaris.................................86
Psilafi................................86

S
Sage...................................14
Seli Gigilou 82,84
Seliniotikos Yiros.............48
Sfakianes Madares 7
Sfakiots 33
Sougia 88
Spilia 74
St George 63
St Pauls........................78,90
Sts Theodore.....................51
Stock-breeding 35

T
Tarra 22,26
Tis Perdikas to Nero........69
Thyme................................14
Tripiti Gorge.....................87
Tzanis Cave......................50

V
Vamvakopoulo 45
Volakias......................20,84
Vryses 80
Vrysi.................................63
Voulisma 51

W
Watermills.........................37
Wedding............................33
White Mountains 7
Wild Goat 15,38
Wine 36
Woodcutter.......................36

X
Xepitiras Cave 6,82
Xyloskalo 7,58

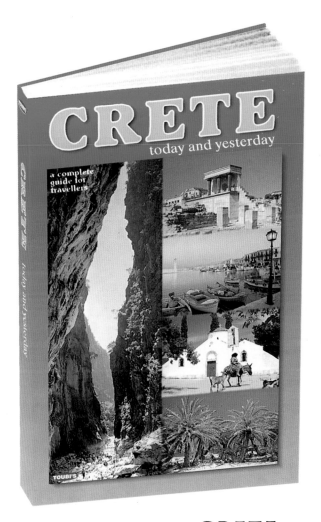

CRETE

*Travellers visiting the rest of CRETE, will
be delighted with our up-to-date tourist guide,
which includes tours of the cities, archaeological
sites and museums, 19 routes on the island,
a detailed map and 302 colour photographs.*

Texts: SOFIA SOULI
Text Editor: SOFIA SOULI
Artistic Editor: NORA DRAMITINOU

Printing-Production: M. Toubis S.A.